# CAVES
## Mysteries Beneath Our Feet

by
**David L. Harrison**

illustrated by
**Cheryl Nathan**

**Boyds Mills Press**

Published by Caroline House
Boyds Mills Press, Inc.
A Highlights Company
815 Church Street
Honesdale, Pennsylvania 18431
Printed in China

U.S.  Cataloging-in-Publication Data
   (Library of Congress Standards)


Harrison, David L.
   Caves : mysteries beneath our feet / by David L. Harrison ;
illustrated by Cheryl Nathan. — 1st ed.
[32] p. : col. ill. ;   cm.
Summary: A basic examination of how caves are formed.
ISBN  1-56397-915-2
1. Caves.  I. Nathan, Cheryl.  II. Title.
551.447  21  2001   CIP    AC
00-112039


First edition, 2001
The text of this book is set in18-point Optima.

10 9 8 7 6 5 4 3 2 1

It was hot,
so hot that most cows
stayed in the shade.
But not Millicent.
She and Farmer Howe's other cows
stood in the hot sun
on a rocky hillside
where some thick bushes grew.

"What a curious way
for cows to behave,"
said Farmer Howe.
He found out why.

His hilly pasture had a hole in it!
Millicent liked the cool air
rushing around her.
She liked being a cool cow.

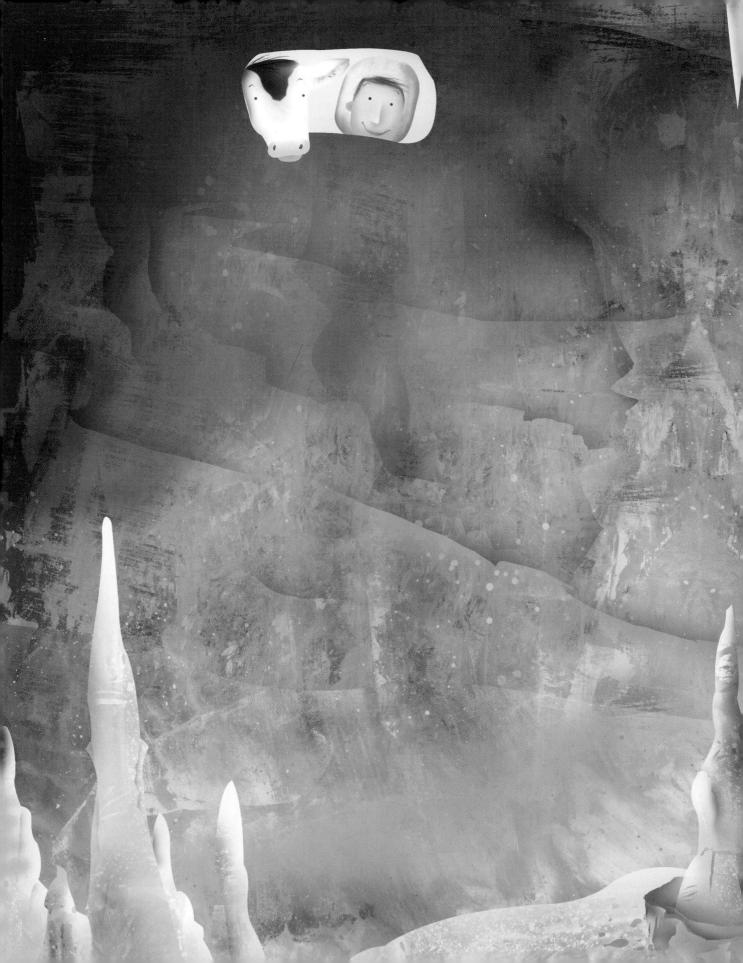

When the surprised farmer
pulled back the bushes,
he found himself looking
into a deep, dark room!
The room was part
of a cave.

How did a cave get under
Farmer Howe's pasture?
The answer involves
raindrops.

When rain falls,
drops splash
into rivers and ponds.
Drops splatter
onto streets and rooftops.
But most drops plop
onto the ground.

Some drops trickle down
through grass and leaves
to pebbles and soil below.

They seep down deeper,
past pebbles and soil,
to rocks as big
as mountains.

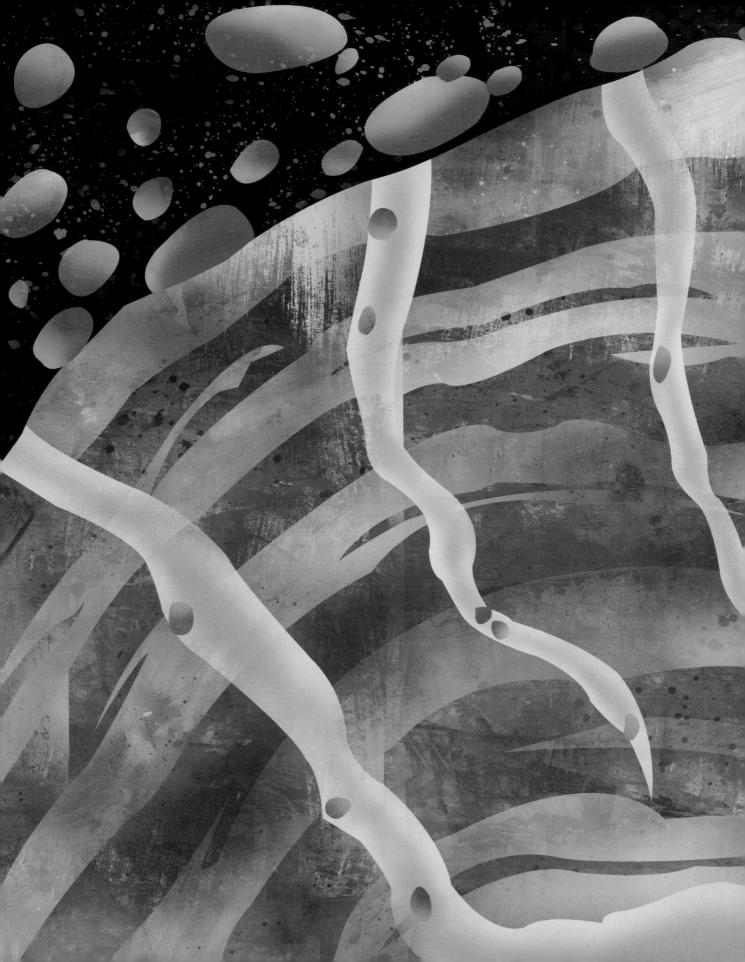

They trickle and seep
into holes and cracks
in the giant rocks.

After enough water
and enough time,
tiny bits of
some kinds of rocks
crumble and wash away.

After many years,
no one knows how many,
some cracks grow
into tunnels and rooms
inside the huge rocks.
They become caves
like the ones Millicent found
in Farmer Howe's pasture.

Some caves form strange
and wonderful decorations
that look like lily pads.
Or ice on a pond.
Waterfalls.
Draperies.
Flowers.
Pearls.
Popcorn.

Water helps form
the decorations, too.
Drops seep into a cave
and hang on the ceiling.
When they evaporate,
the bits of rock they carry
are left behind.

Drop by drop,
small rings grow
on the ceiling.
Bit by bit,
the rings grow
into straws and cones.

The straws and cones
grow bigger and longer.
When they hang down
like stone icicles,
we call them
stalactites (sta-LAC-tites).

Some drops drip
and plink onto the floor.
Plink by plink,
their loads grow
into small bumps
on the floor.

The bumps grow
bigger and taller.
When they reach up
toward the ceiling,
we call them
stalagmites (sta-LAG-mites).

Many animals
spend time in caves.
Most famous is the bat.
In some caves,
bats sleep away the day
upside down,
clinging from ceilings.

At night bats fly out
to find food.
We are glad they do.
Each year hungry bats
eat billions of gnats
and mosquitoes.

Swallows and other birds
may build nests
in the mouth of a cave.
It is a quiet, shady place
to raise their babies.

Raccoons wander
In and out.
Deer stop by.

Foxes, rabbits,
skunks, and rats
come and go,
sniffing for food
or a place to hide.

Spiders hunt crickets.
Salamanders hunt spiders.
Fish and crayfish
hunt insects
in cool cave streams.

But true cave dwellers
live back so far that light
never reaches them
and few visitors
disturb their peace.

True cave dwellers are blind.
They have no need for eyes.
They have no need for color,
so many are clear or white.

White crickets
and white centipedes
feel their way
in the dark,
searching for food.

Hungry blind beetles
scratch in the loose earth.
Spiders hunt on foot.
White crayfish creep
through pools and streams.

Blind fish
no bigger
than your hand
are clear enough
to see through.

Life in a cave
is a constant search
for something to eat.
Sometimes floods
carry in fresh supplies.

Weeds and roots,
leaves and twigs,
and tiny animals
from the soil
are all food
for hungry dwellers
in the dark.
Not a speck is wasted.

When we visit a cave,
we must be careful.
A cave is a community.
Every creature
and every thing in it
is important.

If we touch a stalactite,
we may change forever
the way it grows.

If we step on a cricket,
we may upset
the balance of life.

It is up to us
to protect our caves
and all the creatures
that dwell there.

Farmer Howe's cows
knew nothing of caves.
They just wanted to be cool.
Like us, they lived
on the surface of the earth.

But below the surface,
down deep where rocks
can be as big as mountains,
lies another world.
An amazing world.
The world of caves.

# AUTHOR'S NOTE

Howe Caverns, mentioned in this book, was discovered in the Schoharie Valley in New York State in 1842. But most caves have not yet been discovered. Scientists believe there may be more than fifty thousand limestone caves in North America. Imagine how exciting it would be to push aside a bush and find yourself staring into a great hole in the ground! Caves have been discovered by Native Americans, explorers, miners, hunters, children, dogs, and, of course, Millicent the cow.

There are also other kinds of caves you can learn about. Sometimes when volcanoes erupt, great rivers of molten rock called lava flow down the sides of the mountain until they cool back into rock. Ice caves may form in glaciers, the giant sheets of ice that cover some of the coldest places on earth. Wind and rain and freezing and thawing can carve caves high up in the faces of mountain walls. Along the rugged seashores, the mighty pounding of the ocean sometimes cuts shallow caves into the rocks. There are even caves that happen by accident when an earthquake or landslide causes boulders to pile up against one another and form rooms and tunnels that lead nowhere.

After reading this book, I hope you will want to learn more about the wonderful world of limestone caves. There is so much to say about caves that no one book can hold all the information. That is why I am suggesting other good books on this subject.

**—David L. Harrison**

# FURTHER READING:

Gibbons, Gail. *Caves and Caverns*, Harcourt Brace & Co., 1996 (paperback), 1999 (hardcover).

Greenberg, Judith. *Caves*, Raintree Steck-Vaughn Publishers, 1990.

Gunzi, Christiane. *Cave Life: A Close-Up Look at the Natural World of a Cave*, Dorling Kindersley, 1993.

Knapp, Brian. *Cave*, Grolier Educational Coporation, (Series: Land Shapes), 1993.

Kramer, Stephen. *Caves*, Carolrhoda Books, Inc., 1995

Morris, Neil. *Caves*, Crabtree Publishing Co., 1995.

Siebert, Diane. *Cave*, HarperCollins Juvenile books, 2000.